Rustic Wedding FLORALS

Colorful flowers in simple containers are perfect for a rustic wedding that is elegant yet casual. These DIY projects show how easy and affordable it can be to arrange your own floral decorations, using buckets, baskets, bottles, jars, jugs, and other items. Burlap ribbon, lace, and jute twine make great accents.

LEISURE ARTS, INC. • Maumelle, Arkansas

Trellis Wreath

SHOPPING LIST

- ☐ garden trellis (ours is 54" high x $16^{1}/_{2}$" wide)
- ☐ 14" diameter grapevine wreath
- ☐ floral bush with 5 large roses, a rosebud, and hydrangea blossoms
- ☐ small berry floral stems with leaves and multiple spikes of berries (we used 14 spikes)
- ☐ 2 yards of 6" wide burlap ribbon
- ☐ 5" x $15^{1}/_{2}$" pre-made blank sign
- ☐ white chalk marker
- ☐ grey chalk-finish spray paint
- ☐ floral wire
- ☐ wire cutters
- ☐ tracing paper
- ☐ dressmaker's tracing paper
- ☐ clear acrylic spray sealer
- ☐ hot glue gun and glue sticks

To make the Trellis Wreath:

1. To make the bow, measure out 12" from one end of the burlap ribbon; gather the ribbon between your fingers. Measure out 12" again, gather, and bring the gathers to meet the first gathered point, forming a loop; hold the gathered points together. Twist the ribbon all the way over, measure out 12", gather, and bring the gathers to meet the gathered point, forming a second loop; hold the gathered points together. Make 2 more loops in the same manner. Tightly wrap a floral wire length around the gathers to secure the bow. Trim the ribbon ends as desired.
2. For the sign, spray paint the sign grey; allow to dry. Trace the pattern (page 24) onto tracing paper. Transfer the pattern to the sign with dressmaker's tracing paper. Write over the design with the chalk marker. Once the chalk is dry, spray the sign with sealer.
3. Cut the berry floral stems into individual spikes. Cut the flowers from the bush. Arrange the flowers into an arch shape on the wreath. Use floral wire to attach the flowers to the wreath. Use floral wire to attach the berry spikes around the flowers. Glue elements in place as necessary.
4. Use floral wire to attach the bow to the wreath above the floral elements. Use floral wire to attach the sign to the wreath. Use floral wire to attach the wreath to the trellis.

Wedding

Birdcage

SHOPPING LIST

- ☐ metal birdcage (our birdcage is 14" high)
- ☐ 4-6 assorted succulent stems
- ☐ 13-15 lavender spikes
- ☐ 2" wide lace
- ☐ floral foam disc to fit in birdcage or floral foam ball cut in half to fit in birdcage
- ☐ preserved moss
- ☐ floral pins
- ☐ hot glue gun and glue sticks

To make the Birdcage:

1. Glue the floral foam to the birdcage bottom. Cover the foam with moss, securing with floral pins as necessary.
2. Insert the succulent and lavender stems into the foam.
3. Glue the lace around the birdcage as desired.

Tossing Bouquet

SHOPPING LIST

- ☐ 12-16 assorted flower stems (we used ranuculus, peonies, roses, and a dahlia)
- ☐ 8-10 assorted greenery stems (we used succulents and dusty miller)
- ☐ 3-5 assorted berry stems
- ☐ 3-5 assorted twig stems
- ☐ 7/8 yard of 2 1/2" wide wire-edged linen ribbon
- ☐ 1 3/4" diameter thick cardboard tube (shipping tube, wrapping paper tube, etc.)
- ☐ jute twine
- ☐ floral wire
- ☐ wire cutters
- ☐ hot glue gun and glue sticks

To make the Bouquet:

1. Trim the tube to 6" long. Gluing at the ends and overlapping with each wrap, wrap the tube with the linen ribbon. Gluing at the ends and criss-crossing over the ribbon, wrap the tube with the jute twine.
2. Gather the flowers, greenery, berry, and twig stems tightly in your hand. Arrange the bouquet as desired. Tightly wire the stems together just below the lowest leaf or berry. Slip the bouquet into the ribbon-covered tube; trim any stems that extend beyond the tube. If the bouquet seems a bit loose, add a thin bead of hot glue along the tube top edge to hold the bouquet in place.

Peony Basket

SHOPPING LIST

- ☐ wire basket with 3 galvanized buckets and a handle
- ☐ 3 peony stems, each with 2 large open flowers and a smaller budding flower
- ☐ 30" of $1^1/_2$" wide double-faced satin ribbon
- ☐ $3^1/_2$" wide unfinished wooden heart tag
- ☐ 4 yards of jute twine
- ☐ chalk-finish spray paint (white and grey)
- ☐ clear acrylic spray sealer
- ☐ silver marker
- ☐ preserved moss
- ☐ floral pins
- ☐ floral foam
- ☐ wire cutters
- ☐ painter's tape
- ☐ hot glue gun and glue sticks

To make the Basket:

1. Wrap painter's tape around the upper $1^1/_2$" of each bucket. Spray the buckets white (below the tape); remove the tape. Spray the wood heart white. Spray the basket grey. When dry, spray all items with several coats of clear sealer; allow to dry.
2. Cut floral foam to fit in each bucket. Glue the foam in each bucket. Cover the foam with moss, securing with floral pins as necessary. Insert a peony stem into each bucket, trimming the stem as necessary.
3. Wrap the basket handle with twine, gluing the twine ends on the bottom of the handle. Tie a ribbon bow to the basket handle.
4. Write "Love" with the silver marker on the painted heart.
5. Tie the tag to the basket with twine. Place the buckets in the basket.

Caution: Never leave burning candles unattended.

Aisle Bouquet

SHOPPING LIST

- ☐ 6" galvanized bucket
- ☐ 20" length of 3½" wide burlap/lace ribbon
- ☐ 1½ yards of 2½" wide wire-edged burlap ribbon
- ☐ floral bush with flowers, leaves, grassy stems, and berry stems
- ☐ floral foam
- ☐ preserved moss
- ☐ floral pins
- ☐ hot glue gun and glue sticks

To make the Bouquet:

1. Wrap the burlap/lace ribbon around the bucket; glue in place.
2. Cut the floral foam to fit in the bucket. Glue the foam in the bucket. Cover the foam with moss, securing with floral pins as necessary. Insert the floral bush into the foam center, trimming the main stem as necessary. Spread and arrange the stems as desired.
3. Slip the burlap ribbon through the bucket handle. Tie a bow about 8" above the handle. Trim the ribbon ends as desired.

Hanging Bottles

Let your wedding flowers sway gently in the breeze, creating a romantic atmosphere. Just place a few flower stems in an upcycled soda bottle. Tie a doubled length of jute twine (about 4 yards) around the bottle neck (a drop of hot glue secures the twine) and hang the bottle from a tree branch. If you are using fresh flowers, add a small amount of water to the bottle.

Hanging Bouquet

SHOPPING LIST

- ☐ mixed flower and greenery floral bush
- ☐ quart-size canning jar with jar ring
- ☐ 14" length of 1 3/4" wide lace
- ☐ 5 yards of jute twine
- ☐ 1 cup river stones
- ☐ garden shepherd's hook
- ☐ white chalk-finish spray paint
- ☐ clear acrylic spray sealer
- ☐ wire cutters
- ☐ hot glue gun and glue sticks

To make the Hanging Bouquet:

1. Remove the jar ring from the jar. Spray paint the shepherd's hook and the jar ring white. When dry, spray both items with several coats of clear sealer; allow to dry.
2. Wrap the lace around the jar; glue in place. Replace the jar ring on the jar. Add the river stones to the jar. Cut the flower and grass stems from the floral bush. Gather the flowers and grasses in your hand, arranging them as desired. Place the gathered flowers and grasses in the jar, pushing the stems into the river stones.
3. Cut the twine in half. Folding the lengths in half, tie the twine around the jar mouth, knotting on each side. Glue the knots to the jar. Tie the ends into a bow 12" above the jar lid.
4. Insert the shepherd's hook into the ground, making sure it is secure and stable. Hang the jar from the hook.

Hydrangea Monogram

SHOPPING LIST

- ☐ 18" high unfinished wood letter
- ☐ 2-3 hydrangea flower heads
- ☐ 1 1/4 yards of 1 1/2" wide reversible satin wire-edged ribbon
- ☐ spray paint in desired color
- ☐ hot glue gun and glue sticks

To make the Monogram:

1. Spray paint the letter, being sure to cover the edges. Allow to dry.
2. Trim each blossom from the hydrangea heads. Overlapping for a full look, glue each blossom to the letter.
3. For the hanger, slip the ribbon around/through the letter and tie a bow about 6" above the letter.

Bundled Mason Jars

SHOPPING LIST

- ☐ 3 quart-size canning jars with jar rings
- ☐ 9 Gerbera daisies
- ☐ maidenhair fern bush
- ☐ ivory spray paint
- ☐ $1\frac{1}{2}$ cups floral stones/river rocks
- ☐ 28" length of $2\frac{1}{2}$" wide wire-edged linen ribbon
- ☐ 3 yards of wired jute cord
- ☐ floral wire
- ☐ wire cutters
- ☐ hot glue gun and glue sticks

To make the Jars:

1. Remove the jar rings and spray paint; allow to dry. Glue the jars together in a triangle shape. Replace the rings on the jars.
2. Wrap the linen ribbon around the jars; glue in place. Wrap the jute cord around the jars 3 times, knot at the front, and coil the ends around a pencil.
3. Place $\frac{1}{2}$ cup of stones in each jar. Cut the fern fronds from the bush. Place 7-9 fern fronds in each jar.
4. Holding 3 daisies together, wrap floral wire around the stems, about mid-way down. Insert the daisies in the jars, trimming the stems as necessary.

Love Jug

SHOPPING LIST

- ☐ large brown glass jug (ours is 10$^1/_2$" high)
- ☐ daisy and baby's breath flower stems
- ☐ 2 cork heart-shaped tags
- ☐ chalkboard cardstock
- ☐ white/gold bakers twine
- ☐ white chalk marker
- ☐ craft glue

To make the Arrangement:

1. Cut 2 chalkboard cardstock hearts about $^1/_4$" smaller on all sides than the cork tags. Use the chalk marker to write the desired word or phrase on each chalkboard heart. Glue the chalkboard hearts to the cork hearts.
2. Tie the tags to the jug with bakers twine. Place the flowers in the jug.

Painted Pitcher

Check out your local thrift store for unconventional "vases." Spray paint, simple mixed blooms, and eucalyptus stems transform a sad little pitcher into a sweet centerpiece.

Caution: Never leave burning candles unattended.

Tulips & Lavender in Citrus

SHOPPING LIST

- ☐ 2 gallon clear glass jar
- ☐ 9 large peach tulips with long stems
- ☐ 36 lavender spikes with long stems
- ☐ 1$^{5}/_{8}$ yards of 2" wide wire-edged linen ribbon
- ☐ fresh oranges, lemons, and limes
- ☐ floral wire
- ☐ wire cutters

To make the Arrangement:

1. Gather the tulips and lavender spikes in your hand, arranging the flowers as desired. Wrap floral wire around the stems below the lavender spikes. Place the flowers in the jar, trimming stems as necessary.
2. Slice the oranges, lemons, and limes into $^{1}/_{4}$" slices. Arrange the slices around the flower stems in the jar. Fill the jar with water. Tie a ribbon bow around the mouth of the jar; trim the ends as desired.

Twig Vases

SHOPPING LIST

- ☐ glass cylinder vases (we used 8$^{1}/_{2}$" and 10$^{1}/_{2}$" high vases)
- ☐ bundle of curly willow twigs
- ☐ flower-shaped floating candles
- ☐ acrylic water mix
- ☐ garden pruners to cut willow twigs

To make the Vases:

1. For each vase, cut several twigs about 1" shorter than the vase.
2. Follow the manufacturer's instructions to add about 1"-1$^{1}/_{2}$" acrylic water and twigs to the vases. Once the "water" has hardened, fill the vases with tap water and place the candles on the twigs.

Caution: Never leave burning candles unattended.

Wildflower & Grasses Wine Bottles

Spread some wildflower love! Wrap the neck of deep green wine bottles with jute cord. Add simple wildflower and grasses floral stems to complete this sweet look.

Planter

SHOPPING LIST

- ☐ square galvanized container that will hold four 4" clay pots
- ☐ four 4" clay pots
- ☐ preserved moss
- ☐ jute twine
- ☐ black chalkboard cardstock
- ☐ black chalkboard paint
- ☐ 1" wide foam brush
- ☐ 4 plant pokes
- ☐ white chalk marker
- ☐ 4 desired plants and potting soil
- ☐ craft glue

To make the Planter:

1. Paint the rim and the inside of each pot with the chalkboard paint; allow to dry.
2. Place a plant in each pot, adding potting soil as necessary. Cover the soil with preserved moss.
3. Cut a cardstock piece the same size as the sign area of the each plant poke. Use the chalk marker to add a dotted border and to write wedding related words and phrases. Glue each cardstock piece to a plant poke. Tie a twine bow around each plant poke.
4. Arrange the pots in the galvanized container. Fill in the areas between the pots with preserved moss. Place the plant pokes in the pots.

Monogram Basket

SHOPPING LIST

- ☐ fabric-lined basket (ours is 7 3/4" x 14" x 8")
- ☐ scrapbook paper
- ☐ 8" high papier-mâché letter
- ☐ large autumnal floral bush with flowers, leaves, and seed pods (our bush has 22 flowers)
- ☐ floral foam
- ☐ preserved moss
- ☐ wood skewer
- ☐ floral pins
- ☐ decoupage glue
- ☐ 1" foam brush
- ☐ hot glue gun and glue sticks

To make the Basket:

1. Place the letter right side down on the wrong side of the scrapbook paper. Draw around the letter and cut out. Use decoupage glue to adhere the paper letter to the papier-mâché letter; allow to dry. Hot glue the skewer to the back of the letter near the bottom.
2. Cut a 2" high piece of floral foam to fit snuggly in the basket. Place the foam in the basket and cover with moss, securing the moss with floral pins as necessary.
3. Angling the flowers toward the basket back, insert the floral bush into the foam near the center of the basket. Insert the letter at the basket front.

Caution: Never leave burning candles unattended.

Lavender Jars

SHOPPING LIST

For each jar:

- ☐ green pint-size canning jar
- ☐ 4" diameter birch coaster
- ☐ 17-20 lavender spikes
- ☐ 10" length of $1^{9}/_{16}$" wide white lace
- ☐ 2 yards of jute twine
- ☐ hot glue gun and glue sticks

To make the Jar:

1. Wrap the lace around the jar mouth; glue in place. Cut the twine length in half. Holding both lengths together, wrap the twine around the jar, over the lace, twice. Tie the twine in a bow and trim the ends.
2. Glue the jar to the birch coaster. Place the lavender spikes in the jar.

Burlap-Wrapped Vase

SHOPPING LIST

- ☐ $7^1/_4$" high x $3^1/_4$" diameter clear glass cylinder vase
- ☐ 4" diameter birch coaster
- ☐ 8 sunflower stems, about 4" diameter each (individual stems or cut from a floral bush)
- ☐ 13" length of $3^1/_2$" wide burlap ribbon
- ☐ $2^3/_4$ yards jute twine
- ☐ $1^1/_2$" diameter silver concho
- ☐ 1.75 lb bag of stone granules or sand
- ☐ floral wire
- ☐ hot glue gun and glue sticks

To make the Vase:

1. Cut four 6" lengths of twine. Thread all 4 lengths through the concho. Referring to the photo and gluing the ends in place, wrap the twine lengths on each side of the concho with a 9" length of twine.
2. Wrap the burlap ribbon around the vase; glue in place. Wrap the remaining twine around the vase 4 times; glue in place. Glue the concho to the vase. Glue the vase to the birch coaster.
3. Gather the sunflowers in your hand and arrange as desired, pulling a few stems up slightly higher than the others. Wrap the stems with a floral wire length. Insert the flowers in the vase. Pour the stone granules in the vase around the stems.

Caution: Never leave burning candles unattended.

Pattern Wedding

Production Team: Product Development Director: Anna L. Andrews; Designer – Kelly Reider; Contributing Designers – Kim Hamblin and Becky Werle; Technical Technical Writer – Mary Sullivan Hutcheson; Technical Associate – Jean Lewis; Editorial Writer – Susan Frantz Wiles; Senior Graphic Artist – Lora Puls; Graphic Artist – Cailen Cochran; Photostylist – Lori Wenger; Photographer – Jason Masters.